D0462863

Teen Sex

Risks and Consequences

By Julie K. Endersbe, MEd

Consultant:
Jennifer A. Oliphant, MPH
Research Fellow and Community Outreach Coordinator
National Teen Pregnancy Prevention Research Center
University of Minnesota

Perspectives on Healthy Sexuality

LifeMatters
an imprint of Capstone Press
Mankato, Minnesota

LifeMatters books are published by Capstone Press
818 North Willow Street • Mankato, Minnesota 56001
http://www.capstone-press.com

Printed in the United States of America

Library of Congress Cataloging-in-Publication Data
Endersbe, Julie.
    Teen sex : risks and consequences / by Julie Endersbe.
        p.   cm. — (Perspectives on healthy sexuality)
    Includes bibliographical references and index.
    Summary: Outlines the risks to teenagers involved in sexual
    activity, including pregnancy, sexually transmitted diseases, and
    date rape, as well as options available to teenagers deciding
    whether or not to be sexually active.
    ISBN 0-7368-0272-X (book). — ISBN 0-7368-0293-2 (series)
    1. Teenagers—Sexual behavior Juvenile literature. 2. Teenage
    pregnancy Juvenile literature. 3. Sexually transmitted diseases
    Juvenile literature. 4. Dating violence Juvenile literature. [1.
    Sex instruction for youth. 2. Youth—Sexual behavior.] I. Title.
    II. Series: Endersbe, Julie. Perspectives on healthy sexuality.
    HQ27 .E53 2000
    306.7´0835—dc21   99-29238
                                                           CIP

Staff Credits
Anne Heller, editor; Adam Lazar, designer; Heidi Schoof, photo researcher

Photo Credits
Cover: ©PhotoDisc/Barbara Penoyar
©Digital Visions/Medical Icons, 28
FPG International/©Telegraph Colour Library, 15
©Index Stock Photography, Inc/6, 23, 32, 48, 49
International Stock Photo/©Christopher Morris, 9
Unicorn Stock Photos/©Karen Holsinger Mullen, 18; ©Eric R. Berndt, 10
Uniphoto Picture Agency/37, 56; ©S.H. Begleiter, 43; ©Bob Daemmrich, 55
Visuals Unlimited/©SIU, 27; ©Jeff Greenberg, 40; ©Mark S. Skalny, 47

A 0 9 8 7 6 5 4 3 2 1

Table of Contents

Chapter Overview

The word *sex* has many definitions.

Many teens engage in sexual intercourse while they are in high school. About one in five teens, however, choose not to have sex.

Teens face many risks when they are sexually active. Pregnancy, infections, or emotional pressures are some of these risks.

Peer pressure, fear of violence, and changes in the family may influence a teen's decisions about sex.

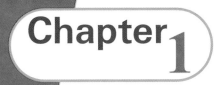

Chapter 1

Teen Sex— Is Everybody Doing It?

The word *sex* has many meanings. It can mean being male or female. Sex may mean reproducing, or having a baby. The longing to be physically close to someone is sexual desire. Usually sex refers to sexual intercourse. Some people call intercourse "having sex." It can be confusing when a word has more than one meaning. This is especially true of the word *sex*.

In this book, *sex* refers to sexual intercourse or sexual closeness. This includes vaginal, anal, or oral intercourse.

My mom gave me the sex talk when I was 15. She had checked out a book about menstruation for me when I was 10. But I don't remember talking about it much.

Kaye, Age 19

When we learned about sex in school, some things were missing. Like we didn't learn how normal sexual desire is when you are growing up. So all the messages my body was sending me were puzzling. When I was a sophomore, I was dating a senior. I was struggling with my limits. My mom must've noticed it. She asked me if I wanted to talk about it. So we talked.

She said, "Kaye, what's going on with your body is normal. Everyone has feelings of sexual desire. It's hard to know whether to give way to your feelings. I just want you to know you can talk with me anytime about your choices."

That really opened up my relationship with my mom. We talked a lot. She helped me to sort out my feelings. She helped me come to my own decision that the best choice for me was to wait to have sex.

One million teens become pregnant each year.

Three million teens acquire an STD every year.

The Reality of Sex

The reality is that many teens are sexually active. More than half of all teens engage in sexual intercourse before age 18. Sex may come with some risks and consequences, however.

Sex can bring pleasure and closeness. It also can involve risks. For example, pregnancy and sexually transmitted diseases (STDs) are risks of sex.

Teens face pressures that can create other risks. Teens are learning to adjust to more responsibilities. Some teens begin working. School becomes more challenging. Also, a teen's body is changing in order to be able to have children. This is a normal part of life. It is not normal, however, for a 12-year-old to have a baby. A 12-year-old isn't ready to parent a child.

Myth: Everybody in high school is sexually active.

Fact: About 75 percent of 15-year-olds, 60 percent of 16-year-olds, and 45 percent of 17-year-olds choose not to be sexually active. By age 18, about 35 percent choose not be sexually active. About 20 percent of 19-year-olds choose not to be active.

How Teens Learn About Sex

Sexuality can be a difficult topic for some people to discuss. People in many other countries are open when talking about sex. Many people in the United States are not so open. Often parents have difficulty talking openly and honestly with their children about sex. Consequently, teens may get information about sex from undependable sources.

Teens get much of their information about sex from their friends. This information is often not accurate. In addition, many people believe the media sends unhealthy messages about sex. Advertisers use sex to sell products. Television uses sex to attract viewers. As a result, children and teens get slanted messages about sexuality.

What Teens Learn About Gender

Society teaches many things about gender. Gender means being male or female. For example, gifts for a newborn baby usually reflect the gender of the baby. A girl may receive a baby doll. People rarely think of giving a doll to a boy. Children learn from the gifts they receive. Little girls learn to practice being a mommy.

Many people tend to picture parenting as a female job. Teen pregnancy facts are reported as female statistics. More females than males take parenting and family living classes in high school. Females often receive mixed messages about their roles. On the one hand, they learn they should be responsible for the family. On the other hand, they are encouraged to be sexy and beautiful.

Society encourages boys to be tough. Boys often are taught not to cry or show emotions when they are hurt. Males receive few positive messages about preparing for fathering or caretaking. The absence of these messages can be hurtful to a boy's development. Boys often aren't allowed time to develop fathering skills. Some people believe the emphasis on being tough encourages males to be sexually active. It may give boys the message that they become men by engaging in early sexual intercourse.

My friends were always talkin' about sex. They couldn't believe I hadn't done it. Sure, I was curious, but I really hadn't dated anyone I wanted to have sex with. My friends talk like sex is so common. They like to talk about it all the time. We were at a party, and they were pushing me and this friend together.

We ended upstairs in bed. I felt like I was just getting it over. The sex thing certainly wasn't anything special. It felt good and all, but it wasn't what I had expected. I would do it differently if I had the chance.

William, Age 18

Influences on Sexual Activity

Many things influence sexual activity among teens. Peers can pressure teens into early sexual activity. Some youth engage in sex because they fear rejection if they don't do it. Others may fear their partner will be physically or sexually violent if they don't willingly engage in sex.

Since the early 1970s, sexual intercourse among teens has increased about 20 percent.

Many experts believe changes in the family influence a teen's sexual activity. The changes in the family may affect how kids are parented. Teens have less consistent adult contact. Some parents do not define clear boundaries or aren't available for their children when needed.

Some youth are less connected in their communities than in the past. In turn, these youth have lost positive adult role models. With fewer connections to family and community, teens may turn to early sexual involvement.

Points to Consider

What are some influences on a teen's decisions about sex?

Why do you think sex is an uncomfortable topic for many people?

Many teens grow up in poverty. How do you think poverty affects a teen's sexual choices?

Chapter Overview

One million teen girls become pregnant each year. About 50 percent give birth, about 40 percent choose abortion, and a small percent choose adoption.

One-third of pregnant teens do not receive good prenatal care. This increases risks during pregnancy to the unborn baby and to themselves.

Most teen mothers are single and poor. Children who are born in poverty face many risks.

Teens who choose parenting, abortion, or adoption deal with emotional challenges. A decision about a pregnancy can be stressful.

Chapter 2

Teen Pregnancy

Sexual intercourse may involve risks. One risk is the possibility of pregnancy. Unfortunately, few teens talk with their partner about the possibility of pregnancy. This lack of communication may help to explain why 85 percent of teen pregnancies are unplanned. In fact, nearly 900,000 teens become pregnant each year in the United States.

Myth: A young woman can't get pregnant the first time she has sex.

Fact: Half of all teen pregnancies occur within six months after first having intercourse. Twenty percent happen within one month. Pregnancy can even happen whenever sperm are near the vagina.

The Risk of Drugs

Fifty-five percent of teens believe an unplanned pregnancy was the result of having sex while drunk or on drugs. Alcohol and other drugs make it difficult to think clearly. Then teens may not be prepared to protect themselves during sex. They may not have protection such as condoms and spermicides. They may not even remember having sex. Drug use can be a serious risk for sexually active teens.

I never dated much in high school. My first **Jamie, Age 18** real boyfriend was two years older than me. He treated me really nicely. My parents really liked him, too. The only thing I had a hard time with was the pressure to have sex. He told me he loved me after our first date. It seemed really soon. I barely knew him, but he acted like we'd been together for months.

He pressured me for weeks to have sex. I didn't want to. I didn't plan on it. But it happened so fast one day after school. I was kind of in shock because I told him I didn't want to. I was even more surprised when my period didn't come two weeks later. Of course, that freaked him out. I didn't hear from him for a few weeks. My first experience with intercourse wasn't like the movies. It wasn't even close.

The Risk of Pregnancy

If the mother doesn't get good prenatal care during pregnancy, there can be risks to the fetus, or unborn baby. Prenatal care involves regular visits to a doctor. A pregnant woman needs to monitor her diet and get regular exercise. She must avoid all types of drugs to prevent possible harm to the baby.

One-third of all pregnant teens do not receive good prenatal care. Their babies are more likely to weigh too little at birth. Low weight at birth means babies are more likely to have development problems.

The Risk to Children

When teens parent, there may be increased risks for children. Children have daily needs. They need parents who understand how a child grows and develops. They need food, clothing, and a safe place to live. Most importantly, they need parents who give them time, attention, and love. The reality is that most teen parents have a lot of difficulty meeting these needs. Children who don't have these needs met are at risk for many problems.

Fast Fact

Ninety-four percent of teens believe they would stay in school if they were involved in a pregnancy. In fact, about 70 percent eventually finish high school.

The Risk of Single Parenthood

Many teens believe they will marry if a pregnancy occurs. Yet more than three-fourths of births among teens happen outside of marriage. Most teen moms parent alone.

Single parents face risks. Poverty is the greatest risk for a single mother and her child. Seven in ten teen mothers finish high school. They are less likely than their peers, however, to go on to college. Many women who parent alone rely on one income or government assistance. Recently government assistance has become more limited.

Teens who choose to parent face many challenges. It is not an impossible job. It is simply more difficult.

If a person has medical coverage in Canada, abortions are free. Teens are covered under their parent's policy. Parents do not have to be notified if an abortion is performed on a teen. The Ministry of Health in Canada always keeps abortion information confidential. Laws about abortions in the United States vary from state to state. Check with Planned Parenthood or call 1-800-78-PLAN to learn the law in your state.

Choosing Abortion

Abortion poses few risks when done in the early stages of pregnancy. Medical abortions using pills must be done only until the seventh week. A surgical abortion can be performed up to 15 weeks after the start of the last menstrual period. Most abortions in the United States and Canada are done during the first 12 to 15 weeks of pregnancy. After 15 weeks, the health risks of abortion increase.

Nearly 40 percent of U.S. teens and 45 percent of Canadian teens choose abortion to end pregnancy. Ninety-seven percent of women have no complications from abortion. Young women and their partners who choose abortion may or may not have emotional aftereffects. Feelings of guilt, shame, or regret may follow an abortion. The most common feeling women have after an abortion is relief. They usually feel that they made the right decision for themselves.

My girlfriend and I got pregnant about six **Justin, Age 19** months after we started having sex. She always told me everything was safe. She promised me everything would be okay and told me not to worry. I was stupid. I easily could have protected myself, but I didn't. I was lazy.

When we told our parents, they both freaked out. Her mom got pregnant when she was 18, so I suppose it hit her hardest. We had both planned on attending college. I wanted to go away to school. The pregnancy changed our plans for now.

The baby is due any day. We are still talking about adoption. We've seen a counselor and even have some parents in mind. I don't know how we'll feel once the baby is born. Money will matter. Plus we aren't getting along too well anymore. This wasn't supposed to happen. I'm not ready to deal with this yet.

Choosing Adoption

A very small percentage of teens choose adoption. Adoption occurs after the birth of the baby. The mother, and the father when possible, sign the Consent to Adopt form. This is a legal document through which parents give up rights to their baby.

Many teens can't imagine sending their baby into another person's home. Others realize their own limitations. They understand other families are waiting for babies. Independent, or open, adoptions even allow the teen mother to choose a family for her baby. Perhaps the hardest part is dealing with the emotions involved in the decision.

Points to Consider

What is one reason that teens may not always engage in protected sex?

How can teens think more about the risks of pregnancy before becoming sexually active?

Describe the risks for teens who choose to parent a child.

Are you surprised that relief is the most common feeling women have after an abortion? If so, why?

Chapter Overview

People can get an STD by having sex even once with someone who has the disease.

Many people notice no symptoms, or evidence of a problem, when they have an STD.

The viruses that cause AIDS, genital warts, genital herpes, and hepatitis B all stay in the body for life.

Different bacteria cause chlamydia, gonorrhea, PID, and syphilis. These diseases can be cured with antibiotics and rarely cause permanent damage when treated early.

Choosing not to have sexual contact is the only sure way to prevent STDs.

Chapter 3

Sexually Transmitted Diseases

STDs are sexually transmitted diseases. Sometimes they are called STIs, or sexually transmitted infections. STDs are acquired from an infected person during genital contact or vaginal, anal, or oral intercourse. An STD can be acquired by having sex just once with someone who is infected.

It is hard to tell when someone else has an STD. Many STDs have no symptoms, or evidence of the disease. Often people who are infected don't know they have a disease. They are not aware they can pass it on. This is why STDs are such a high risk to teens who are sexually active.

Myth vs. Fact

Myth: AIDS is a disease that only homosexual, or gay, people get.

Fact: HIV, the virus that causes AIDS, is most commonly spread between heterosexuals.

About three million teens acquire an STD each year. These diseases can cause problems for the rest of a person's life. Some STDs can be treated and cured. Other STDs cannot be cured but can be treated. Some STDs that aren't treated can cause permanent damage or death.

HIV and AIDS

Human immunodeficiency virus (HIV) causes AIDS, which stands for acquired immunodeficiency syndrome. HIV goes unnoticed for a long time while it destroys the body's immune system. It leaves the body unable to fight germs and disease. Symptoms may not show up for several years after infection with HIV. By that time, a person usually has AIDS, a complex of many diseases.

AIDS is particularly common among young people. One-fifth of all people in the United States who have AIDS are in their 20s. Nearly half of all new AIDS cases are in women between 18 and 24. These people most likely were infected with HIV in their teens.

HIV is usually spread through direct contact with body fluids. Such fluids are blood, semen, vaginal fluids, or breast milk. Intravenous drug users who share needles also can spread the infection.

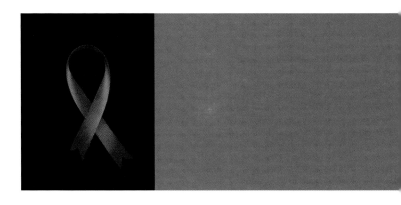

It is important to know how HIV is NOT spread. HIV is not spread through receiving or making blood donations. If donated blood tests positive for HIV, it will not be used. HIV is not spread through casual contact such as wrestling, hugging, shaking hands, or touching another person. Kissing someone on the mouth does not spread HIV. People cannot get HIV by visiting someone in the hospital who is infected. People cannot get HIV from a toilet seat, comb, or doorknob that someone with HIV has touched. A mosquito or bug bite doesn't transmit HIV.

AIDS has no cure. Most people eventually die from one or more diseases against which the body cannot defend itself. Therefore, careful decisions about sexual partners and protected sex are important. Abstinence, or choosing not to engage in sex, is one effective way to avoid HIV. Using condoms, not sharing needles, having only one sexual partner, and using dental dams also help.

Genital Warts
Human papilloma virus (HPV) is the name of a group of viruses that have many different types. Some types of HPV can cause genital warts. Many people who have genital warts do not know they have them.

Some studies show about 15 percent of sexually active teen women are infected with HPV. Like adults, teens can be infected with the HPV strain that can cause cervical cancer.

Did You Know?

If a teen woman engages in one act of unprotected sex with an infected partner, she has:

- a 1 percent chance of getting HIV
- a 30 percent chance of getting genital herpes
- a 50 percent chance of getting gonorrhea

HPV can be treated but not cured. The virus stays in the body for life. The best defense is not to have sexual contact with an infected partner. Latex condoms may help if they cover the infected area.

Genital Herpes

A virus causes genital herpes or HSV II. Usually genital herpes appears as clusters of painful blisters in the genital area. The blisters break and then heal. The sores may reappear many times in the same area. Over time, the sores may lessen. About half of all people with the herpes virus will have only one outbreak. Even so, the virus stays in the body for life.

Genital herpes is usually passed through contact with the broken blisters. It can be passed even without open sores. Usually the virus enters the body through a break in the skin or through the genitals or mouth. The blisters may appear three days to three weeks after infection occurs.

No medication removes the herpes virus, but some medicines help to heal the blisters. The medicines also help to prevent future outbreaks of blisters.

Hepatitis B

A virus also causes hepatitis B. It is passed through vaginal, anal, or oral sex with an infected partner. It is also passed through sharing contaminated needles or other contact with infected blood. Less often hepatitis B can be passed through saliva.

Symptoms appear between one and nine months after infection. Many people have very mild symptoms, and others have no symptoms at all. This infection can cause permanent damage to the liver. Once a person is infected, the virus remains in the body for life.

Hepatitis B is the only STD for which there is a vaccine to prevent it. Everyone should be vaccinated. Teens especially should be vaccinated because they are at very high risk of the disease.

Chlamydia

A bacteria causes chlamydia, a disease more common among teens than adults. Symptoms may show up 7 to 21 days after having sex with an infected partner. One symptom may be a discharge from the penis or vagina. Most women and some men, however, have no symptoms.

Chlamydia is easily treated with antibiotics. If the disease isn't treated, it can lead to damage to the reproductive organs. Sexually active males and females should ask to be tested when they see their doctor. They also should be tested each time they have a new sexual partner. Condoms are effective in preventing chlamydia.

Gonorrhea

A kind of bacteria causes gonorrhea, which is similar to chlamydia. The two diseases have many of the same symptoms. The symptoms can occur within 2 to 21 days after sexual intercourse.

An antibiotic cures gonorrhea. If gonorrhea isn't treated, however, it can cause heart trouble and skin and joint diseases. It can cause blindness in babies born to infected mothers. It also can cause pelvic inflammatory disease (PID).

Pelvic Inflammatory Disease

Pelvic inflammatory disease is a serious infection of a woman's reproductive organs. In the United States, PID is the leading reason that women cannot have children. Chlamydia and gonorrhea are the most common causes of PID.

PID can develop within days or months after infection with an STD. Usually PID occurs when the STD isn't treated right away. PID can be treated successfully with antibiotics if it is found early.

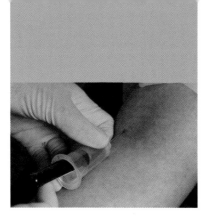

Syphilis

A bacteria causes syphilis, which usually is passed through sexual contact. The bacteria also can enter the body through broken or cut skin.

Syphilis occurs in three stages. The first stage happens 3 to 12 weeks after infection. A sore appears for one to five weeks. The second stage shows up one week to six months after the sore heals. A rash or flu-like symptoms appear in the second stage. If syphilis isn't treated, the major organs are damaged in the third stage. The disease may take more than 20 years to reach the third stage.

Treatment with antibiotics can cure syphilis when it is discovered early. If it is not treated, however, it can damage the heart, brain, or spinal cord. Syphilis can even cause death. It also can cause problems or death in a newborn.

STDs and Pregnancy

It may take time for STDs to be diagnosed. This can be dangerous for a pregnant teen. She can pass an infection to her baby without knowing it while she is pregnant. Some STDs also can be passed to a baby during birth or through breast-feeding. For these reasons, many health care providers test for STDs early in a pregnancy. Most STDs can be treated and not passed on to the baby.

Reducing the Risk

People who are sexually active should be tested at least once a year for STDs. They also should be tested every time they have a new partner. This is the only way to find out about an infection and receive prompt treatment.

Abstaining from, or not having, sex is the most effective means of prevention. Teens who choose to be sexually active should limit the number of sexual partners. It is best to limit the number of partners.

Using protection during sex is another way to prevent STDs. A condom and spermicide should be used just before and during sex. Male or female condoms should be used.

It is important for people to communicate their sexual history to all partners before having sex. When couples know this information, they can choose to avoid the risk of STDs. They can do this by abstaining from sex or using condoms.

Many teens have found other ways to enjoy sex without intercourse. Many avoid the risk of STDs by waiting to become sexually active. Although this can be a difficult choice, it is a healthy one.

Points to Consider

Why do you think so many teens are infected with an STD each year?

Why are very young teens at a higher risk for getting an STD than adults are?

Describe how people can protect themselves from being infected with an STD.

How could schools better teach teens about protection against STDs?

Chapter Overview

Teens with a history of sexual or physical abuse learn difficult messages about sexuality.

Sexual harassment is unwanted or inappropriate jokes, statements, or touch. It happens to many children as early as elementary school age.

Rape is forced sexual intercourse. Date or acquaintance rape is increasingly more common. Both males and females can experience rape.

Victims of rape have physical or emotional effects because of the crime. A counselor or doctor can aid in recovery from the effects.

People can learn ways to prevent dating violence.

Chapter 4

Dating Violence

Dating violence happens when a person is mistreated in a verbal, sexual, or physical manner. It may take the form of sexual harassment, sexual abuse, or sexual assault or rape. A relative, friend, or stranger may be the person who does the mistreating. The violence or mistreatment is always unwanted and is never the victim's fault.

Sexual Harassment

Sexual harassment is unwanted or inappropriate jokes, statements, or touch. Sexual harassment can be inappropriate remarks or jokes about a person's clothing, body, sexual orientation, or behavior. It can be unwanted or repeated requests or pressure for dates. It can be physical behavior of a sexual nature such as patting, touch, or caressing. Sometimes it is unwanted sexual requests or advances. Sexual harassment is a form of abuse.

Both men and women can be sexually harassed. More often, however, females are the targets of sexual harassment. Sexual harassment can happen to people who are not sexually active.

Harassment is all too common. A study was conducted among U.S. high school students. It found two-thirds of the girls had been grabbed, pinched, or touched in a sexual way at school. Forty-two percent of the boys experienced similar harassment. Many children experience harassment in elementary school. Unfortunately, the media sends sexual messages, especially about women, that add to the harassment.

Sexual harassment can be eliminated if people understand it. Setting clear boundaries and limits can help decrease harassment. Many schools and businesses have policies against harassment.

Most teen girls who have intercourse before age 15 report it was forced on them.

Fast Fact

Sexual Abuse

Some people have been sexually abused. Any sexual contact that is forced on people can affect their future relationships and sexual behavior. For example, by ninth grade sexually abused teens are twice as likely to be sexually active as their peers are. Sexual abuse can happen to young children, teens, or even adults. It can affect a person's attitude about sexuality for many years.

Sexual abuse can lower self-esteem and consequently affect how people feel about themselves. Professional counselors can help sexually abused teens to work through their feelings.

Rape

Rape is forced sexual intercourse. A person also can be blackmailed into having sex. Rape can occur when the victim is drunk. By definition, rape is always without the victim's permission.

A stranger sometimes rapes people. More often, however, the rapist is someone the victim knows. Most victims of rape are women.

Rape is a punishable crime, regardless of who the attacker is.

Date or Acquaintance Rape

Date or acquaintance rape means the victim knows his or her attacker. The victim usually trusts the attacker and does not suspect any violence will occur. This puts the victim at a high risk because he or she is unprepared. Some experts think less than 10 percent of date rapes are reported.

Drinking alcohol or using other drugs can increase the risk for dating or sexual violence. Most date rapes occur when drinking has been involved. Physical abuse or sexual assault also can occur. The use of drugs does not excuse a person from losing control and becoming violent.

The Effects of Rape

Victims of rape struggle with feelings about the attack for a long time afterward. Often they have feelings of shame associated with the rape. The victims may blame themselves for not expecting or preventing the rape. They may not be able to feel anger about the attack.

Often victims have other physical and emotional effects after the rape. They may have headaches or nausea. They may be unable to sleep. The victims may feel depressed. Some have anxiety or nightmares about the attack. These effects are often part of rape trauma syndrome. Some victims may develop fear of or strong distaste for sexual intimacy, or closeness. The effects of rape are substantial.

Victims of rape may or may not have chosen to be sexually active before the attack. Rape has nothing to do with a person's decision about sex. Rape is a violent, unwanted attack. It is about power and control for the attacker. The attacker otherwise may not be openly violent.

Preventing Dating Violence

In healthy dating relationships, each partner feels safe and is not pressured. When one partner feels unsafe or pressured, the partner should leave the relationship.

It is important to send clear messages to a partner. Sometimes one partner sends mixed messages to the other partner. For example, one partner may flirt while saying no to having sex. This message is confusing. The other partner may think the message really means yes and may try to have sex anyway. No means no regardless of what else is done or said.

Victims of dating violence can do a number of things.

1. Don't ignore it. Seek help. Contact an abuse shelter, the police, or a school counselor.

2. Don't blame yourself. You are not responsible for another person's behavior. Violence is always the responsibility of the attacker.

3. Know your rights. Sexual harassment, rape, and sexual assault are illegal. There are laws that protect you.

It helps to avoid high-risk situations. Walking or going out alone at night is a risk. Another high-risk situation involves parties where alcohol or other drugs are available. Drugs impair a person's ability to set limits. It is important for people not to let drug use take away their control.

Another way to prevent dating violence is to know the history of a partner. It helps to talk with other people who know the person. Dating a person with an unknown history can be risky. Group dates are a healthy alternative to being alone with some partners. This can prevent being in unsafe situations.

Talking with trusted people can help. Trusted adults can provide advice based on their knowledge or their own experiences. They may be able to help determine whether a relationship has signs of potential abuse.

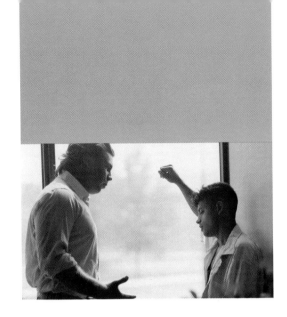

The most important way to prevent dating violence is to think ahead. It helps to have a plan for dealing with situations that may become unsafe.

Points to Consider

How can early sexual or physical abuse affect future dating relationships?

Why do you think rape is a crime that mainly men commit?

What advice would you give a friend who just told you her boyfriend raped her?

What could your school, community, or friends do to help deal with dating violence?

Chapter Overview

Postponing sexual activity can be difficult for teens. They get many confusing messages about sex.

Many teens choose not to have sexual intercourse.

Couples who talk about their sexual limits build respect for each other. They also can work together to establish sexual boundaries.

Teens who are active and involved are less likely to feel pressure to be sexually active. They build confidence in their skills.

Chapter 5

Choosing Not to Have Sex

Teens may feel confused about sex. They find it difficult to resist
sexual activity for many reasons. For one thing, the adolescent body
constantly produces a high level of hormones. These hormones send
strong messages to the body for sexual activity.

The media helps to make sex look attractive, especially to teens. It
sends messages that sex brings a lot of friends and good times. The
media often neglects to address the consequences of sexual activity,
such as an unplanned pregnancy or an STD. Most messages from the
media don't teach people about sexual responsibility. It's tough to
know how to deal with these messages.

Teens have a natural curiosity about sex. Friends or some family members may encourage teens to have sex. These pressures can make it hard to postpone sexual activity.

Teens are not just pressured to have sex. Many teens also are pressured to use alcohol and other drugs. Drugs and sex are a dangerous combination. Drugs impair judgment and make it hard for teens to maintain their limits about sex. Drugs also make it hard to use condoms and other pregnancy prevention methods correctly every time people have sex.

My girlfriend and I have talked a lot about **Andre, Age 18** sex. It's kind of weird because we spend more time talking about it than most people spend doing it. But we've both seen a negative side of sex. My sister got pregnant when she was 16. We have a friend who drinks too much and can't even remember the girls he has sex with.

We have strong feelings for each other. And when we start kissing and stuff, well, it's hard not to take it to the next step. That's why it's good we talk about our limits. I want to go to the Air Force Academy. I want to be a dad someday. But right now I'm just not ready for the risks that come along with having sex.

Myth: Guys have stronger sex drives than women and are always ready to have sex.

Fact: Men have been allowed to express their interest in sex more than women have. However, men and women have equal sex drives.

Choosing Abstinence

Not all teens choose to have sexual intercourse. More than 50 percent of teens have not had sex by age 16. More teens have sex as they get older. Even so, some still choose not to have sex.

Abstinence happens when people choose not to engage in sexual relations. Teens might make this choice because of religious beliefs. Some may choose abstinence because they feel it's healthier. Abstinence is the only totally effective way to avoid pregnancy or an STD. Abstinence costs nothing. It does take careful planning, setting limits, and skill and practice to say no.

A person must think ahead and plan how to deal with sexual pressures. Teens need to decide on their limits. Some teens choose not to date seriously. Others may choose to avoid being alone with their partner. Group dating is a fun way to date without the pressures of sex.

Did You Know?

One in five teens have not had intercourse by the age of 18.

I had been with two other guys before Dimitris. I thought that everybody had sex. But Dimitris is different. He told me up front he didn't want to go all the way. I thought he was just playing, but he's not.

Felicia, Age 19

It's been hard for me. I have strong feelings for Dimitris. I especially want to have sex with him. He is always careful with me. He tells me he loves me and that he doesn't want to do it. He knows what he wants. I really love and respect him. We've found lots of other creative ways to show our love for each other besides having sex.

Partners Talk

Dating is a normal experience for teens. A teen can choose abstinence and still date. Some teens have chosen to be sexually active in the past and then choose abstinence.

It is important that partners talk about their feelings, decisions, and sexual history. Personal issues about sex can be hard to talk about. Sharing their feelings and history allows couples to be honest with each other. This can help a couple work together to have a healthy relationship. Couples who talk about their limits build respect for each other. They can learn to enjoy each other sexually without having intercourse.

Get Active

Keeping busy helps to resist sexual pressure. It helps to be active and find healthy things to do with people with similar beliefs. It helps to get involved. Many teens are active in theater or service groups. Other teens go out for athletics or organized sports like volleyball or swimming. Still others like less organized sports such as inline skating or skateboarding.

Teens who are active build skills. It takes commitment and discipline to be involved. Commitment and discipline are the skills that can help a teen set strong limits about sex. Teens who are involved usually have high self-esteem. They feel good about themselves and their choices.

Points to Consider

What do you think influences teens to be sexually active?

Alcohol and other drugs make it harder for a person to think clearly. How can they affect how teens deal with sex?

How can a couple set sexual limits?

Name five activities you can get involved with in your school or community.

Chapter Overview

The body of most teens is physically ready to be sexually active. Teens must consider many other factors when deciding if they are emotionally ready for sex.

Teens who are ready for sexual intercourse need to communicate with their partner. They need to discuss each other's sexual history and the risks of sex.

Teens must choose methods for preventing pregnancy and STDs that are right for them. A health care professional can provide information about the choices.

Chapter 6

Making the Best Decision

Most teens are physically ready to have sexual intercourse at a young age. However, few are ready to handle the emotional side of a sexual relationship. It can be tough to decide about personal readiness for sex. For example, some religions teach that sex should happen only after marriage. Some people choose not to have sex because of their beliefs. Some people believe it is important to take time to know a person well before having sex. There are many factors to consider about sexual readiness.

Myth: There is something wrong with a guy if he hasn't had sex by the time he is 18.

Fact: Many males choose not to have sex during their teens. It does not mean they are not masculine. Having sex does not make a man.

People know me for a lot of different things. I was captain of the football team, homecoming king, and on the honor roll. I am in the men's choir and act in several plays each year at school. But I do have a reputation. Just about everybody in school knows I haven't had sex yet. It doesn't bother me. I go to middle schools and talk to the students about my choice. I've even spoken at my place of worship about my beliefs.

Adam, Age 18

I am not embarrassed about my choice. Once I made a commitment to myself, it really hasn't been that hard to resist sex. I have great friends. I've done so many great things. I want to try it all, even sex, but not now. Maybe in a few years I'll be ready for the responsibilities of sex.

Indicators of Sexual Readiness

There are some ways other than age that people may know if they are ready for sexual intercourse. In fact, age does not necessarily indicate readiness. People may, however, be emotionally ready. They may feel confident they can handle the feelings surrounding a sexual relationship. A person must have self-confidence to be emotionally ready.

People can know they are sexually ready if they are prepared for the possible consequences or outcomes of sex. For example, a pregnancy can occur. Teens who are ready for sex know how to prevent an unplanned pregnancy.

Another way people know they are sexually ready is if they are able to disclose their sexual history. For example, one partner may have been exposed to an STD. A partner who shares needles during intravenous drug use also could have an STD. The other partner needs to know these things before the couple engages in sexual intercourse.

Finally, people need to decide if their partner is worth it. A teen may fall in love with someone. He or she may plan to be with the person for life. Yet it is impossible to see into the future to know how long the relationship will last. What will the partner do if a pregnancy happens? Will the partner be dependable? Will the partner share the responsibilities for protected sex?

Preventing Pregnancy

Pregnancy happens when a male's sperm fertilizes a female's egg and the egg implants in the wall of the uterus. Most teens want to prevent pregnancy. They usually are not ready to be parents. Therefore, it is important to discuss pregnancy prevention before teens engage in sexual intercourse. Teens who plan ahead are more likely to avoid pregnancy.

There are many reliable ways to prevent pregnancy. A health care professional can prescribe or provide certain types of pregnancy prevention methods. A prescription is necessary for birth control pills. A health care provider must give progestin through a shot or an implant under the skin. Both methods prevent an egg from being released each month. Without an egg, fertilization cannot happen.

Another pregnancy prevention method that requires a prescription is emergency contraceptive pills. These tablets provide an emergency method of preventing implantation of the fertilized egg in the wall of the uterus. They must be taken within 72 hours after unprotected sex or intercourse. Every female who is having intercourse should get a supply of these pills from her doctor just in case.

Other pregnancy prevention methods that do not require a prescription also help to prevent STDs.

Preventing Sexually Transmitted Diseases

Teens who plan ahead are more likely to avoid disease. Couples who are ready to engage in sex for the very first time may not be concerned about STDs. This is because their sexual history may not include any risky behaviors. If either partner has had vaginal, anal, or oral intercourse, STDs may be a concern.

Condoms are a reliable means for preventing STDs for couples who are having vaginal or anal sex. Teens most often use condoms, usually because they are affordable and easily available at stores. Both male and female condoms serve as a barrier during sex. Condoms help prevent exchange of body fluids that carry infection.

Following the directions for proper use of condoms is important. For pregnancy prevention, condoms are most effective when used with spermicides to kill sperm. For STD protection, latex or polyurethane condoms, commonly called "rubbers," should be used. While condoms greatly reduce the chances of getting an STD, they may not protect all areas from STDs. Condoms only cover the penis or protect the walls of the vagina. If condoms are not used properly, they can break or may not collect all of the fluids.

Couples who engage in oral sex also need barriers. Dental dams help to prevent passage of STDs during oral sex. Health care providers and some drugstores have dental dams available. Flavored condoms are another option.

The truth about latex condoms.

Condoms are only effective when used correctly every time people have sex.

It is 10,000 times safer to use a condom during intercourse than not to use one.

When used correctly, condoms are 98 percent effective in preventing pregnancy. When combined with a spermicide, condoms also may reduce the risk of certain STDs.

Points to Consider

What advice would you give a friend who is thinking about having sex with a new partner?

How can teens decide if they are ready for a sexual relationship?

Which method of pregnancy or disease prevention do you think is most effective? Why?

How is honest communication or a reliable type of pregnancy prevention important in a sexual relationship?

Chapter Overview

Sexual responsibility is part of a healthy lifestyle. Reducing risk factors, working to heal past wounds, and building strong relationships are part of a healthy lifestyle.

Teens can build a strong future by finishing their education.

Sexual responsibility involves communication between partners, protected intercourse, and respect for a partner's limits.

Teens may decide to postpone having sexual intercourse until they are ready.

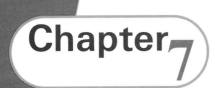

Chapter 7

Your Future—
Making It Work for You

The reality is that many teens are sexually active. Even so, some positive trends have appeared recently. First, the rate of teen pregnancy steadily dropped in the 1990s. This trend may be because teens are choosing to engage in protected sex or to abstain from sex. Second, the U.S. abortion rate is the lowest it has been in more than 20 years.

These statistics indicate that teens are being sexually responsible. Teens who are sexually responsible decrease their risks of pregnancy and STDs. There are many ways in which teens can be sexually responsible.

Reduce Your Risk Factors

Whenever possible, teens can reduce their risk factors. Teens face many risks that don't disappear when they become adults. You can choose to avoid such risks as unprotected sex, drugs, or drinking.

Learn From the Past

Your past helps make you who you are today. Some teens have faced sexual violence or abuse in the past. This can affect current relationships because time alone does not heal some wounds. It helps to talk with someone. A counselor, trusted adult, or therapist can help sort through painful past experiences. Resolving such experiences helps to build strong relationships in the future.

Find an Adult You Can Trust

Trusted adults are an important part of your support system. They can listen and help to advise you through their own life experiences. Often they know where you can get help if you need it.

Surround Yourself With Good Friends

Good friends share fun, trust, honesty, and similar beliefs. It helps to surround yourself with friends who don't pressure you to take risks. Good friends find healthy things to do together and help each other make good choices. They encourage each other to avoid risky behavior such as unprotected sex. They encourage each other to be responsible sexually and in other ways.

Make School a Priority

Finishing school is your ticket to a good standard of living and better paying jobs. Being involved and engaged in school can be a key part of helping you achieve your future goals.

My boyfriend and I talked about having sex for months. We really love each other. We talk about our future together. He wants to be a carpenter and build furniture. I think about being a computer specialist.

Conchita, Age 17

When we made a decision to have sex, we went to our clinic. I got the "shot." The doctor also suggested we use condoms and spermicides every time we have sex. My boyfriend helped me to remember when it was time to go get another shot. He practiced putting on a condom before we needed it.

I talked to my mom about our decision. She talked about all the risks of sex. But she was proud of how responsible we were. I feel good about our choice. We have not had unprotected sex once. We aren't ready to be parents yet, and we don't want an STD.

Prevent STDs and Unplanned Pregnancy

Latex or polyurethane condoms are effective for preventing pregnancy and STDs when used correctly every time you have sex. Here are some tips on using condoms.

1. Use a new condom with every act of sexual intercourse, including vaginal, oral, and anal intercourse.

2. Store condoms in a cool place out of direct sunlight, not in wallets or glove compartments.

3. Check the expiration date.

4. Carefully open the package to avoid ripping or tearing the condom.

5. Use only water-based lubricants, which reduce dryness. Lubricants such as cooking oil, baby oil, hand lotions, or petroleum jelly can cause a condom to break.

6. Put on the male condom while the penis is erect and before sexual contact begins. Slowly unroll the condom over the penis, leaving a half-inch at the tip to collect semen. Pinch the tip to remove any air.

7. While the penis is still erect, hold onto the base of the condom and withdraw the penis immediately after ejaculation. Then hold onto the rim of the condom and slowly withdraw the penis from the condom. Make sure no semen spills.

Myth: Sexual intercourse is the only way to show someone you love him or her.

Fact: Couples have many ways to show love for each other. There are times when all couples may choose to abstain from sex. Couples can show, or "make," love without intercourse.

Talk With Your Partner

Teen partners need to talk. They need to share their sexual history with each other. Teens need to discuss and respect their sexual limits. It is time to end the relationship if your partner doesn't respect your sexual limits.

If you and your partner choose to engage in sex, it is necessary to be responsible. Partners need to practice sexual responsibility together. You can avoid the risks of unprotected sex. You both need to visit a health care professional. That person will help to find the best method of pregnancy and STD prevention for you.

Carefully Decide About Sexual Activity

Teens who are not emotionally ready for sex may struggle with deciding about sexual activity. A teen must consider many factors when deciding about sex. Therefore, it is important to make the decision carefully and thoughtfully.

Many teens choose not to have sex while they are in high school. It helps to weigh the risks of sexual intercourse. It may be a matter of waiting for the right person or the right time. Think about how sexual activity will affect all aspects of your life. Talk about it with a trusted friend.

Take your time when making the decision about sex. The opportunity to have sex will not go away. You can choose to postpone the opportunity.

Points to Consider

What can teens do to reduce their risk factors?

How does resolving painful past experiences help relationships?

Name three ways teens can practice sexual responsibility.

What do you think it takes to make a healthy and responsible relationship?

Glossary

abortion (uh-BOR-shuhn)—a medical procedure that ends a pregnancy

abstinence (AB-sti-nenss)—choosing not to do something; abstinence from sexual activity is an effective way to prevent sexually transmitted diseases.

adoption (uh-DOP-shuhn)—the process through which adults take a child into their family and become the legal parents

egg (EG)—the female reproductive cell; when an egg is fertilized, it develops into a new human being.

fetus (FEE-tuhss)—a baby developing in the uterus from eight weeks after fertilization until birth

gender (JEN-dur)—male or female

genitals (JEN-i-tulz)—sex organs; the male sex organ is the penis and the female sex organ is the clitoris.

penis (PEE-niss)—the male reproductive organ

prenatal care (pree-NAY-tuhl KAIR)—a pregnant woman's regular doctor visits before a baby is born

reproduction (ree-pruh-DUHK-shuhn)—the process through which a male and a female produce a child

sexual intercourse (SEK-shoo-wuhl IN-tur-korss)—penetration of the penis into the vagina

sperm (SPURM)—the male reproductive cell; one sperm is capable of fertilizing a female's egg.

vagina (vuh-JYE-nuh)—the passage that leads to the uterus in females; babies pass through the vagina at birth.

For More Information

Basso, Michael J. *The Underground Guide to Teenage Sexuality: An Essential Handbook for Today's Teens and Parents.* Minneapolis: Fairview Press, 1997.

Endersbe, Julie K. *Healthy Sexuality: What Is It?* Mankato, MN: Capstone Press, 2000.

Kelly, Gary F. *Sex & Sense: A Contemporary Guide for Teenagers.* New York: Barron's, 1993.

Kreiner, Anna. *In Control: Learning to Say No to Sexual Pressure.* New York: Rosen, 1997

Theisen, Michael. *Sexuality: Challenges and Choices.* Winona, MN: St. Mary's Press, 1996.

Useful Addresses and Internet Sites

National Abortion Federation
1755 Massachusetts Avenue Northwest,
Suite 600
Washington, DC 20036
Hotline 1-800-772-9100

National AIDS Hotline
P.O. Box 13827
Research Triangle Park, NC 27709-3827
1-800-342-AIDS

Planned Parenthood Federation of America
810 Seventh Avenue
New York, NY 10019
1-800-230-7526
www.plannedparenthood.org

Planned Parenthood Federation of Canada
1 Nicholas Street, Suite 430
Ottawa, ON K1N 7B7
CANADA
www.ppfc.ca

Pro-Choice Action Network
1675 West 8th Avenue, Suite 219
Vancouver, BC V6J 1V2
CANADA
www.prochoiceconncetion.com

Advocates for Youth
www.advocatesforyouth.org
Information for teens on preventing HIV, teen
pregnancy, and more

Kids Help Hotline in Canada
kidshelp.sympatico.ca
Information, tips, links, and more that
Canadian youth can use in facing life's
challenges

Sex, Etc.
www.sxetc.org
A teen-produced website that deals with health
and sexuality issues

Teen Center
www.wholefamily.com/kidteencenter
Straight talk about pregnancy, sex, drugs, etc.

Index